Deep Joy

40 Meditations for Your Journey

BETH-SARAH WRIGHT

Master Design Publishing,
an imprint of Master Design Marketing, LLC
32 N Gould St
Sheridan, WY 82801
www.MasterDesign.org

ISBN 978-1-941512-64-7

Printed in the USA.

These things
I have spoken to you,
that my joy
may be in you, and that
your joy may be full.
John 15:11

Contents

An Introduction to Joy

On Ash Wednesday of 2020, I wrote a blog on joy for 40 days (BethSarahWright. com). Joy, because my soul was yearning for it. Joy, because I knew happiness was not sustainable, and I wanted more. Joy, because I had tasted pain and was grateful for the relief of healing and restoration. Joy, because I know that was not possible without God. Joy, because it is hardy and durable and can withstand the vicissitudes of life.

However, on February 14, 2020, no one knew what would befall us in just a few weeks. Writing about joy amid such devastation, trauma, and pain was a complex journey. Some days, I struggled to find the joy, the light, the hope, and even asked publicly, "Shall I continue?" I only received affirmations: "Yes, you must continue." The journey began as one to seek out joy, but it transformed into new questions, investigation, and curiosity about the depth of joy—especially joy in a period of such suffering. But even amid that darkness, light pierced through with remarkable acts of kindness, human connection, and generosity of spirit. It was, ironically, the ideal incubator to examine joy. Deep joy knows both the sting of suffering and the salve of healing. Deep joy is an anchor. Deep joy knows peace.

The 40 meditations on this journey to deep joy are inspired from that period during the pandemic. The contagion that plagued us then is in many ways replaced by other contagions—viruses of divisiveness and blatant disregard for human dignity. But hope remains. Restoration is possible. Joy is within reach. Some meditations remain just as they were in 2020. Others have been gently massaged to pertain to now. Each meditation concludes with a question or thought for you to journal, discuss or ponder.

God promises that joy may be in us when we abide in God's love and ways. I continue to sing this joy song, intentionally seeking out and enacting an element of joy each day in my life and punctuating it with a declaration: "Things that bring me joy!" With God, our joy is inside us, coursing through our veins, never wavering and always complete.

Join me on this journey to deep joy!

A Journey into Joy

Today begins a journey into joy. That word has been whispering to me. I seek it. I desire it. I yearn for it. I hope for it. It eludes me, and I want to taste some joy. We could all use more joy in our lives. For the next 40 days, I invite you to join me on this journey into joy. Each day, I will meditate on some element of joy to gain a deeper understanding of it. I will focus on things that bring me joy ... an image ... a quote ... a poem.... What are your thoughts about joy? What brings you joy? Not fleeting happiness. Not cheer or gladness. Rather, a sustainable, abiding joy in the face of all that life brings us—journey with me.

> *"May the God of hope fill you with all joy and peace in believing, so that by the power of the Holy Spirit you may abound in hope."*
> – Romans 15:13 (RSV)

I'll begin with a poem from my book, *Becoming Who I Am*, "A Pilgrimage to Joy":

Encounter. Entangle. Enrage.

Enquire. Enlist. Entreat.

Engage. Enact. Endure.

Enshrine. Enable. Enliven.

Endeavor. Enough.

En**JOY!**

Why do you want to embark on a journey to joy?

Joy in Beginnings

As I watched the sunrise this morning, I was reminded of the joy in new beginnings. Joy in the possibilities, the potential, the hope, the promise of something new. The joy in choosing a new way of being, a new practice, a thought. We have this opportunity when granted another day, another hour, another minute, another second of life.

> *"No dark fate determines the future. We do. Each day and each moment, we are able to create and recreate our lives and the very quality of human life on our planet. This is the POWER we wield."*
> – Dalai Lama XIV, *The Book of Joy: Lasting Happiness in a Changing World*

What new way are you choosing today?

Meaningful Joy

What is it like to wake up with joy? For some, it is no problem. For some, we wake up with a heaviness. Burdened with the details and responsibilities of our lives. Sometimes weighed down by what is happening in the world around us. Recently, I have found myself wanting to avoid the news, being profoundly affected by world events, and the inhumanity in humanity, and the fact that hurting people hurt people. Yet, I seek joy in sadness or suffering or pain. I am learning that waking up with joy means having meaning and choosing joy. There must be intentionality in the equation.

I choose joy. I choose this day to make a difference. I choose this day to be the difference. I choose God's will. I choose kindness and compassion. I choose good for others. I choose to become "a reservoir of joy, an oasis of peace, a pool of serenity that can ripple out to all around you" (Archbishop Desmond Tutu in *The Book of Joy: Lasting Happiness in a Changing World*).

What do you choose today? What is meaningful to you? I pray it brings you and others a deep and abiding joy.

When asked what it is like to wake up with joy, the Dalai Lama said:

> *"I set my intention for the day: that this day should be meaningful. Meaningful means, if possible, serve and help others. If not possible, then at least not to harm others. That's a meaningful day."*

_____

How do you wake up with joy?

_____

Joy Comes in the Morning!

"Weeping may tarry for a night, but joy comes in the morning."

– Psalm 30:5 (RSV)

By far, this is one of my favorite Bible quotations. It is a promise of hope. Even in the fog of sorrow, waterfalls of tears, moans of pain, or mountains of obstacles, there is a promise that joy will come in the morning. These dark nights can be long. World history tells us that darkness can last four hundred years ... or even more. But joy is still promised to us. What does this say about the rhythm of life? Or the way God works?

No matter what, no matter how long, no matter how deep, no matter how wounding ... hope and joy still remain a possibility. Hold on. Wait and see. Taste the joy in the morning.

"Sometimes when you're in a dark place, you think you've been buried, but you've actually been planted." BLOOM!

– Christine Caine

_____

What are you hoping for in the morning?

_____

Joy comes with living an authentic life ... one aligned with our purpose. Every day, we are faced with temptations—moments when we have urgings, feelings, and voices that entice us away from our true purpose, what we know is right for us. They bring us moments of fleeting satisfaction or short-lived gratification. Sometimes, we hurt others with these choices. Sometimes, we hurt ourselves.

We feel authentic joy when we live into our purpose and listen to the quiet, still voice inside us. That voice can withstand discomfort or change, even in dark moments. It is the sound of the genuine! That voice knows what is right on a visceral level. Right for us. Right for others. Right for the world. We know it when we hear it. I pray when we do that, we listen to it ... for joy's sake!

> *"There is something in every one of you that waits and listens for the sound of the genuine in yourself. It is the only true guide you will ever have. And if you cannot hear it, you will all of your life spend your days on the ends of strings that somebody else pulls."*
>
> – Howard Thurman, in his 1980 commencement address at Spelman College

What does the sound of the genuine in you sound like?

The Color of Joy

"More than that, we rejoice in our sufferings, knowing that suffering produces endurance, and endurance produces character, and character produces hope, and hope does not put us to shame because God's love has been poured into our hearts through the Holy Spirit who has been given to us."
– Romans 5:3–5 (RSV)

Joy is indeed a complex emotion. It can span from wonder before something astonishing and admirable, to amusement, gratitude, ecstasy, and bliss, and even to unhealthy jubilation or *schadenfreude*—relishing in someone else's suffering. People often view it as closely related to happiness or contentment … something distant from pain. But joy is intimately connected to pain. Pain and suffering do not take away one's joy. It enriches it.

When my now husband and I were dating, he gave me a mixed tape entitled "Blue" on one side, with all these slow, sorrowful songs, and the other side entitled "Red," with more up-tempo, highly rhythmic songs. He said together, they produce Purple, the color of joy.

Joy is satisfaction and peace amid the pain. Joy is seeing that you are not alone in pain. As the saying goes, "Pain is inevitable; suffering is optional." Joy is being reassured that God is with you always. Joy knows we are all connected. Joy is in shifting your perspective to see opportunity in the pain. Opportunity for deepened learning or opportunities to grow or change. God does not cause everything, but God can use everything!

I pray we can see the joy even in our dark moments.
Let's embrace the colors of joy!

Acceptance + Patience = Joy

"So much of what causes heartache is our wanting things to be different than they are."
– Dalai Lama XIV, *The Book of Joy: Lasting Happiness in a Changing World*

For a myriad of reasons, we often feel like we must have everything under control. We think we ought to be "perfect" on day one. We want immediate success. We want no disruptions, no obstacles, no impediments. Then, when it doesn't quite turn out how we want, we feel frustrated, anxious, angry, disappointed ... and the list goes on. No joy.

What if we were to accept ourselves as we are? Accept our fallible human nature. Accept those things we cannot control. Be patient with ourselves as we grow, learn, and mature. Be patient with ourselves as we make inroads to new paths, aspirations, and goals. After all, "If you look really closely, most overnight success stories took a long time" (Steve Jobs).

Joy comes when we are patient with ourselves and patient with others and can accept and embrace where we are right now in this moment. Is there any surprise that in many twelve-step recovery programs, including Emotions Anonymous, the Serenity Prayer is a resource to encourage those who are struggling and seeking emotional wellness?

"God, grant me the serenity to accept the things I cannot change, the courage to change the things I can, and the wisdom to know the difference."
– Reinhold Niebuhr (1932)

What do you need to change? What do you need to accept?

What's Joyful about Worry, Anxiety, and Stress?

"Worry is a way for your brain to handle problems in order to keep you safe. ... It's only when we get stuck thinking about a problem that worry stops being functional."
– Dr. Luana Marques, associate professor of psychiatry at Harvard Medical School; president of the Anxiety and Depression Association of America

I read a wonderful article distinguishing the differences between worry, stress, and anxiety. Of course, I was immediately drawn to it because I worry, stress, and get anxious—about work, my family, and the world around us. In many ways, one could ask, what is there not to be worried, stressed, or anxious about?

But all of these emotions impact my ability to feel joy. In fact, like powerful and persistent clouds of smoke, they billow and pulse as they darken my soul. So, where is the joy in all of this? This article reminded me that there is actual use in worry, anxiety, and stress, which gives me joy.

"In small doses, worry, stress, and anxiety can be positive forces in our lives."
– Emma Pattee in "The Difference Between Worry, Stress and Anxiety"

They can help lead to change, create new thoughts, and even reveal new directions. We only need to shift the temptation to be paralyzed by worry to leveraging our stress and anxiety for good. The article suggests budgeting our worry time—consciously limiting the time we allow ourselves to worry.

Joy is rooted in intentionality. Yes, we may worry, for it seems to be human. But let's be intentional about limiting that worry, for ultimately, we don't need it.

> *"Then Jesus said to his disciples: 'Therefore I tell you, do not worry about your life, what you will eat; or about your body, what you will wear. For life is more than food, and the body more than clothes. Consider the ravens: They do not sow or reap, they have no storeroom or barn; yet God feeds them. And how much more valuable you are than birds! Who of you by worrying can add a single hour to your life?'"*
>
> *– Luke 12:22–25 (NIV)*

What can you worry less about today?

The Joy in Talking

"Community takes the 'C' out of Crazy!" –
A stranger whom I had met shared this gem with me.
I never got her name.

At first, I didn't know what this woman meant by this comment, but it stuck with me because I was astonished by how much we don't share our hard journeys in the community with one another. Too often, we are scared and ashamed, embarrassed to share our darkest, most vulnerable moments. Afraid we will be considered "crazy," "weak," "not a strong enough believer," "a mistake," "not worthy," "not good enough," "unforgivable," or "overly dramatic."But it is in sharing and talking that we can shed light in the darkness, and healing, forgiveness, friendship, a new way out, and a resolution can be revealed. Human beings are complex and varied, and whatever it is that silences our tongues has been done or experienced before. We are not alone, and remembering that brings me joy.

What if we were to talk about it? Build community around it? Even if that community is you and one other person, a stranger with a listening ear, or frankly, a piece of paper that will absorb the ink of a focused pen controlled by you, writing your story, and writing a new ending. How do we begin to share? It could be as simple as saying, "Help."

I pray that we each muster up the courage to tell our stories. To not be afraid. To not think that we are alone. To not think we are the only ones ever to experience what we feel. To not think we are so different. There is a community. It is a human community. *Ubuntu*—the South African philosophy meaning, "I am because we are."

"Dare to be vulnerable. Denial and shame thrive in silence. Choose not to be silent. Don't keep it to

yourself. Empower yourself and others by embracing your story."
– Dr. Beth-Sarah Wright, *10 Things I Wish I Knew about Depression Before It Almost Took My Life*

How do you share your story?

_____

Joy When It's Joyless

"We cannot cure the world of sorrows, but we can choose to live in joy."

– Joseph Campbell

It is fair to say that we are bombarded by many images of fear, uncertainty, and even sorrow. So, how do we live in joy in a world that seems a little joyless?

We can accept the reality. We can breathe in peace and breathe out any anxiety. We can do everything in our power to prepare, make a difference, address, tackle, respond to, and resolve what we choose to do now. We can appreciate the presence of the persons we love around us and love them fiercely. We can pray. We can laugh. We can hug. We can feel. We can be kind. We can share. We can choose joy.

Today, let us choose joy.

What do you choose today?

reJOYce!

"Though the cherry trees don't blossom and the strawberries don't ripen, though the apples are worm eaten and the wheat fields stunted, though sheep pens are sleepless and the cattle barns are empty, I'm singing joyful praise to GOD. I'm turning cart-wheels of joy to my Savior God. Counting on God's Rule to prevail, I take heart and gain strength. I run like a deer. I feel like I'm king of the mountain!"
– Habakkuk 3:17–19 (MSG)

Enough said!

*"The lotus flower: its characteristics are a perfect analogy for the human condition. Even when its roots are in the dirtiest waters, the **Lotus** produces the most beautiful **flower**."*
— Ellen Wahl

How do you bloom when in darkness?

13

Day 12

And Was Made Woman ... Joy!

There is joy in being a woman. I love being a woman and pray we all value what that means every day.

A poem I wrote, entitled, "And Was Made Woman. . ." from *Becoming Who I Am*

> (Our Belief)
> We believe in our God
> Our Mother-Father God
> Our refuge
> Our stronghold,
> Our rock
>
> We honor our elders leaning on the lives of our sisters in Christ,
> We lean on Sarah, Mary, Esther, Naomi, Ruth;
> We lean on our enslaved foremothers, our freedom fighters, our
>   trailblazers.
> We learn from them, we carry their wisdom on our shoulders, and we
>   pass their powerful legacy onto our daughters.
>
> We support, encourage, embrace, raise up, build up, hold up our sons,
>   our men
> Let me say that again!
> We support, encourage, embrace, raise up, build up, hold up our sons,
>   our men.
>
> For we know that the work of Moses, Noah, Jesus, and many others,
> Yesterday, today and tomorrow
> Has been strengthened by the power and presence of women.
> Remember we were "Last at the cross, first at the tomb."

14

(Our Oblation)
We embrace, believe in and nurture our children, our youth.
We are mothers, blood mothers, other mothers; stepmothers, adoptive
    mothers;
Aunties, grandmas, great grandmas, big sisters;
We love, encourage and support our children for haven't you heard?
"Out of the mouths of babes and sucklings, praise has been perfected!"

We know we are sinners
We forgive ourselves
We forgive ourselves
We forgive others
We let go and we let God.

We believe in God's justice
We believe in God's justice
We believe in God's justice.

(Our Beauty)
Our lips shout for joy when we sing praises to the Lord!
We sing
We laugh
We drink tea!
We love our food!
We weep, we break our hearts, we hug, we hope, we heal.
We dance
We sway our hips
We walk in that certain kind of way!
With a little sass, a little shimmer!
We strut with God's confidence running up our spines!

We are beautiful!
We are beautiful!
We are beautiful!

(Our Prayer)

When we are afraid, when we are worried, when we are faced with life's valleys;

When the waters have come up to our necks and we sink deep in the mire, where there is no foothold. . .

We look to the young teenaged girl over 2 thousand years ago, who was visited by an Angel and told that she would be a mother to a son who would be called the Christ; we look to this young mother who, with a deep and abiding faith, simply said in response to this news,

"be it unto me according to thy word"

Thy will be done!

And we pray, yes, we pray!

We pray with a vengeance; we become prayer warriors.

We pray with a boldness because we know that if we

"Ask it will be given, if we search we will find and if we knock, the door will be opened!"

For with God nothing is impossible!

We affirm the Holy Spirit in our lives guiding our every move, our every decision, our every waking moment, we give our lives over to God.

Praise be to God, Praise be to God, Praise be to God!

Lord, we thank You for women, we thank You for their lives, we thank You for their strength and their perseverance.

We ask God's blessings on our continued journey as women so that we may be renewed spirits and live with a newness and sweetness of life.

Which women do you admire and why?

Joy in Work ... It Begins with Purpose

"You don't find your purpose, you build it."
– John Coleman, *Harvard Business Review*

Work is one of those areas where people either experience great joy, seek more joy, or question joy altogether. We wonder if this is where we are best suited to be. Or, we wonder if our gifts are being best used or if our gifts are being used at all. We wonder, if we find just the right job, our lives will be so drastically different, and it will be pure joy to go to work, and that will end any frustration or unfulfillment.

Do we need to shift our perspective? What if we were to create joy in our work? Not wait for it to appear or be revealed. No matter what work we do.

I read in a recent issue of the *Harvard Business Review* that having purpose in our work can make all the difference. Purpose? "Most of us feel we've never found it, we've lost it, or in some way falling short." But the upshot of the article was that there is no magic purpose we will discover under the proverbial rock. Rather, we must intentionally create purpose and joy in our work.

Almost any work can possess a remarkable purpose. We need to **infuse** it with purpose. We need to give it meaning. And in doing so, we may discover new joy.

What purpose are you building?

Joy in Purpose(s)

"Most of us will have multiple sources of purpose in our lives."

– John Coleman, *Harvard Business Review*

Ever think you only have one purpose in life? Ever wait for your one purpose to be revealed? What if we were to shift that whole way of thinking to embrace the idea that we actually have multiple purposes? We have different purposes—strengths, gifts, and talents—to use and leverage.

It gives me great joy to consider the possibility that we have multiple dimensions. We don't have to limit ourselves to an elusive single purpose. This is a common misconception as we search for meaning and purpose.

We may be waiting for this one magical panacea. This one thing that we devote our lives to—this one purpose we must embody to be whole. When we think of those we admire, who we are convinced have found their purpose, we confine them to one dimension.

On the contrary, we are versatile as human beings. We have multiple strengths—yes, some more pronounced than others. But we have much to share, and we need to embrace that. Yes, Martin Luther King Jr. was a civil rights leader and icon. He was also a husband, a father, a brother, and a friend.

Let us explore all of who we are. Let us share all of who we are with the world. That gives me great joy!

> *"There is one body, but it has many parts. But all its many parts make up one body."*
>
> – *1 Corinthians 12:12 (NIRV)*

What new gifts have you discovered in you?

Purpose in Faith ... Joy!

"For God gave us a spirit not of fear but of power and love and self-control."

– 2 Timothy 1:7 (ESV)

Central to my purpose as a believer in God and a follower of Christ is exercising faith, even the size of a mustard seed. But faith with work. A partnership with God that believes that God can make gold out of garbage and silk out of scar tissue, all as we live into our purpose(s), strengths, and gifts. Using our minds, our skills, and our reason. This God creates wonderful reversals, where teenagers conquer giants, a newborn can change the world, and a young woman can discover inner courage, choose not to remain silent, and deliver her whole people ... for such a time as this.

This gives me joy! Even in the whirlwind of emotions that swirl around us, God works.

Let's partner in faith and work. It is a sacred partnership, after all. Thanks be to God!

How are you purpose-driven?

Stand Strong in Joy. No Panic.

"Panic causes tunnel vision. Calm acceptance of danger allows us to more easily assess the situation and see the options."

– Simon Sinek

Gracious God, we pray for calm, level-headed, informed decision-making, impassioned care and thought, safety and protection for humanity, acceptance and adaptability, courage and bravery, and love and respect for others.

We pray to be more like palm trees that stand tall and bend and flex in the face of hurricane winds. With You, joy and all things are possible. Thanks be to God.

_____

How do you remain calm?

_____

Joy in Gratitude

"There is a calmness to a life lived in gratitude, a quiet joy."

– Ralph H. Blum

Gratitude. A pillar of joy.

I feel such a deepened gratitude for life, faith in humanity, faith in love, and more than anything, gratitude for God's presence, even in moments that seem ungodly. No need to know the details, know this ... never let go of the hope. Be open to being astonished. I never want to forget this feeling of pure gratitude right now. This is joy.

What are you grateful for?

Seek Out the Joy

"Pay attention. Be astonished. Tell about it. I was surrounded by the beautiful crying forth of the ideas of God."

– Mary Oliver

On Ash Wednesday of 2020, I told myself that I would write a meditation on a journey to joy each day. Like the rest of the world, I could have never imagined the chaos and uncertainty of the time that unfolded. It wasn't easy to meditate on joy each day. Today still brings its own challenges, for sure! But I am reminded of the remarkable ways God works, and I remain committed to seeking joy. God never promised there would never be trials or sufferings. God promised His steady presence amid it all.

This is what I wrote in 2020 when our children were sent home from their various colleges and we were quarantined. I still find the words meaningful for today:

"So, I continue to seek it out. I am joyful my family is home with me. Joyful to see their faces and just know they are close and we can hunker down together. I am joyful for the surge of prayer and kindness and thoughtfulness and togetherness and unexpected beauty around the world even with the mandated social distancing and fear. I am joyful to know that even the closed schools will continue to provide food for those families whose only meal may be the one they get at school. 'Count it all joy,' the Bible says in James 1:2–4. Count it ALL joy."

God provides us all we need to survive and thrive, no matter the circumstance. Pay attention to the way God works.

"Count it all joy, my brethren, when you meet various trials, for you know that the testing of your faith produces steadfastness. And let steadfastness have

its full effect, that you may be perfect and complete, lacking in nothing."

– James 1:2–4 (RSV)

_____

Where do you see joy?

_____

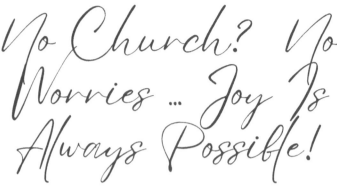

No Church? No Worries ... Joy Is Always Possible!

"Make sure you don't take things for granted and go slack in working for the common good; share what you have with others. God takes particular pleasure in acts of worship—a different kind of 'sacrifice'—that take place in the kitchen and workplace and on the streets."

– Hebrews 13:16 (MSG)

Remember when churches were closed during the pandemic? Then we could not go to church. Today, some of us have not returned. Today, some of us choose no longer to attend church. But not to worry. Joy is not confined to the walls of churches.

Joy is free to reign in our acts of worship. I am reminded by God's words in Hebrews that God takes pleasure in our acts of worship for the common good when we share with others and when we can bring joy to the world. And there are so many ways to do that! I love the opportunities for innovation that are emerging in these unusual times. Let's do this!

During the pandemic, my husband shared these words of encouragement when we could not gather for worship. They continue to be relevant today.

What you can do rather than go to church this morning!

1. Have worship at home with your family.

2. Take a walk and think about God's goodness to you.

3. Make a list of folks who could use a kind and encouraging word and call or text them.

4. Call someone you struggle to love and just say, "I was just thinking about you."

5. Start reading the Bible.

6. Make an online donation to an organization that is doing important work.

7. Commit to pray for those in the healthcare space for the rest of this pandemic.

8. Turn off the TV; turn on the music that touches your soul.

9. Commit to using all of your social media to post positive, edifying posts.

10. Go to the store for someone.

11. What would you add to this list?

You see church can't actually be canceled; it can only adapt. God bless you. Wash your hands!
– Bishop Robert Wright,
Episcopal Bishop of the Diocese of Atlanta

_____

How do you worship?

_____

A Splash of Color in a Monochrome World . . . Joy!

"Mere color can speak to the soul in a thousand different ways."

– Oscar Wilde

This was the image outside my window this morning. It brought me such joy. A bright red robin perched on a wooden fence with a tall lush verdant pine tree giving her shade.

From 2020, the first day of remote working and teleworking:

This is day one for many of us teleworking, or having children home doing remote learning. This is a new day with new adjustments. Thank God we have the capacity to be adaptable. This is a source of major discomfort, uncertainty, and perhaps even devastation for many. Concerns about the next paycheck or questions about childcare. For some, this is a mere inconvenience. Still, this new norm has urged us to think creatively, be innovative, and discover new possibilities. The Honorable Robert Nesta Marley once said, "You never know how strong you are until being strong is the only choice you have."Gracious God, help us to be some color in someone else's life today.

How do you express color?

Joy in Connection

From 2020, when we were figuring out how to stay close in social distancing:

We're all feeling it to some degree. The necessary strain of keeping apart from each other. Yet some of us, regardless of the severe warnings, still yearn to be close to others and risk our own and others' health. Just look to some crowded beaches in popular spring break destinations.

Of all times, in this climate of heightened anxiety, being with others is what many of us so desperately seek and, truth be told, need. I see my teenagers upset they are not with their friends, feeling cooped up in the house and disappointed they will more than likely live out the rest of their freshman year of college at home. Many are feeling the pang of loneliness and depression, and anxiety may be settling in.

But in all this, we are probably all closer together than we've been in recent times as families, local communities, and even as a country. We are praying for loved ones and strangers. Calling and texting folks we haven't spoken with in ages. Creating ways to build community even when we are not physically together in spiritual ways (drive-in churches!), and innovative ways for learning and education. We are sharing tips for homeschooling, even sharing silly adult games on social media to keep our minds occupied and bring some needed laughter. Think of all the ways we are connecting even while we are being asked to stay apart.

We are remarkable! Let us remember the ways we are banding together now, transcending national and international boundaries and race and age and gender and religion and economic status and even politics.

This is joyful news!

How do you stay close?

Pray without Ceasing ... Joy!

"Rejoice always, pray without ceasing, give thanks in all circumstances; for this is the will of God in Christ Jesus for you."

– 1 Thessalonians 5:16–18 (ESV)

With every breaking news update, every alert ping on my phone, and every news broadcast, this Scripture brings me hope and joy. Prayer. Prayers of gratitude. Prayers for help. Prayers for calm. Prayers for wisdom in all that we do. Prayers for those making decisions that affect people's lives and livelihoods. Prayers for the sick. Prayers for the caregivers. Prayers for those still serving others. Prayers for the dying. Prayers for those who have died. Prayers for those they leave behind. Prayers for hope. Prayers for a way through. Prayers for God's presence every step of the way.

Thanks be to God! Thanks be to God!

How do you pray?

Joy in Imagination

The following prayer is from an "unknown" author I had discovered at the height of the pandemic. While it is a prayer specifically about the COVID-19 virus, as I read it now, I could easily replace it with the virus of divisiveness that seems to be plaguing us today. Be imaginative with me and say this prayer with the following in mind: that this prayer be one for peace and justice today and the ability to respect the dignity of all human beings. Prayer is central to deep joy. It grounds us. It comforts us. It empowers us. It allows us to let our requests be known … and be at peace.

Let us pray:

Lord, Jesus Christ, you traveled through towns and villages, curing every disease and illness. At your command, the sick was made well. Come to our aid now, in the midst of the global spread of the coronavirus, so that we may experience your healing love.

Heal those who are sick with the virus. May they regain their strength and health through quality medical care.

Heal us from our fear, which prevents nations from working together and neighbors from helping one another.

Heal us from our pride, which can make us claim invulnerability to a disease that knows no borders.

Lord, Jesus Christ, healer of all, stay by our side in this time of uncertainty and sorrow.

Be with those who have died from the virus. May they be at rest with you in your eternal peace.

Be with the families of those who are sick or have died. As they worry and grieve, defend them from illness and despair. May they know your peace.

Be with the doctors, nurses, researchers, and all medical professionals who seek to heal and help those affected and who put themselves at risk in the process. May they know your protection and peace.

Be with the leaders of all nations. Give them the foresight to act with charity and concern for the well-being of the people they are meant to serve. Give them the wisdom to invest in long-term solutions that will help prepare for or prevent future outbreaks. May they know your peace, as they work together to achieve it on Earth.

Whether we are home or abroad, surrounded by many people suffering from this illness or only a few, Lord, Jesus Christ, stay with us as we endure and mourn, persist and prepare. In place of our anxiety, give us your peace.

Lord, Jesus Christ, heal us.

– Author unknown

How do you imagine the world?

Joy in a Wake-Up Call?

I read in the *New York Times* the findings of the World Happiness Report showing Finland being named the number one country in the world in terms of happiness. The authors questioned the timeliness of this report in the time of COVID-19. Ultimately, they concluded, that there are lessons the U.S., whose ranking dropped to number eighteen, may need to heed.

> *"It is likely to be the case that we will come through this better if we hold our social connections together. We can't fight this epidemic just at the individual level. We need a lot of shared action."*
> – Jeffrey D. Sachs, professor at Columbia University and director of the UN Sustainable Development Solutions Network that publishes the annual World Happiness Report

At the same time, I received a text from a friend saying, "This virus stuff, I believe, is giving our citizens a wake-up call; despite the political competition for the soul of our nation, we are recognizing the need to come together to pray and work to defeat this common enemy." I pray we use this time in our homes as an opportunity to pause, reflect, and rethink who we are—as individuals, as families, as local communities, and as a nation. I deeply pray there is something good and joyful to discover here. ... May God help us to wake up and see anew.

_____

What is waking you up now?

_____

Joy in Movement!

I am a dancer in my soul. I love to move and to let rhythms vibrate throughout my body. It brings me great joy! I love to move and walk every day, rain or shine, in the darkness and in the light. Walking brings me great joy! My soul loves to run. I love to hear myself breathe and listen to the rhythmic crunch of pebbles beneath my running shoes. My body responds with all sorts of ailments—bunions, plantar fasciitis, pain coursing through my feet and hips. I need to move. I started to swim every day in the early mornings. The water is meditative and calming. Swimming brings me great joy. I know that movement is medicine for me. I know that I need it the way I need water to survive. It keeps me balanced. It grounds me. It brings me great joy!

A psychiatrist once told me that he has a prescription that many of his patients never seem to fill. "What is it?" I asked. He said, "Go for a walk."

What is your relationship to movement?

Apocalyptic Joy

"For at one time you were darkness, but now you are light in the Lord. Walk as children of light (for the fruit of light is found in all that is good and right and true)."

– Ephesians 5:8–14 (NIV)

My husband and I are fans of post-apocalyptic movies. Are you? We're always curious as to why they look so dark and barren. But it doesn't have to be, does it? Did you know that the word "apocalypse" means in Greek simply this: "a revealing, an unveiling, or unfolding of things not previously known." There is hope and illumination, and dare I say joy in that!

One could say we lived in an apocalypse during the pandemic, witnessing extraordinary acts of kindness and thoughtfulness in those dark and fearful times! Impromptu concerts by professional artists and by musically inclined neighbors! A two-day-long virtual dance party hosted by popular DJ D'Nice that gathered thousands of people in joy and song! Touching moments of virtual family gatherings. Spontaneous applause thanking healthcare workers working tirelessly to save people's lives. Remember? The light was breaking through the darkness in remarkable ways.

And we continue. We don't need a pandemic to be the light. The apocalyptic time is now. It is our opportunity now to shine the light. Let us reveal the light. Let us unveil the right and true acts. Let us unfold the good in the world right now. Let us be the light and bring joy!

_____

What new things are unfolding for you?

_____

From 2020:

High school and college seniors face a totally unexpected and disappointing senior year. The Summer Olympics may be postponed. I can't imagine the disappointment athletes must feel after years of training, anticipation, and hope.

My daughter is heartbroken she will be finishing her freshman year at NYU at home. She just got accepted into a fabulous theater program in India for the summer, which will probably be postponed until next year, and she is devastated. My son at boarding school is so sad he is missing out on his boarding experience, which he absolutely LOVES, having chosen this path three years ago.

So, what do we do with this unavoidable disappointment in the times of COVID-19? What do we do with any heart-wrenching disappointment?

We pause. We grieve. We pivot. We look for opportunity. We seek out learning. We don't lose hope.

> *"God can do anything, you know—far more than you could ever imagine or guess or request in your wildest dreams!"*
>
> *– Ephesians 3:20 (MSG)*

How do you face disappointment?

Hold Steady in Joy!

"Words kill, words give life; they're either poison or fruit—you choose."

– Proverbs 18:21 (MSG)

As we enter another election year, we're hearing a lot. Different points of view. Different opinions. Differing findings. Differing advice. Lots of different words. Take care in the words you allow to land on your heart and lips. They impact our joy.

Be wise as serpents and harmless as doves. Hold steady. Listen wisely. Be curious. Pay attention. Remain tethered to your faith. You might be surprised by how you hear and what you say.

How do you hold steady?

The Joy of Doing Nothing!

From 2020, when it was quieter and we began discovering new things about our way of being:

> **"Don't underestimate the value of doing nothing, of just going along, listening to all the things you can't hear and not bothering."**
>
> – *Pooh's Little Instruction Book*

I've really been enJOYing seeing all the newfound joy discoveries people are sharing during this unexpected but welcomed time at home. I've seen the most touching ways neighbors are being more neighborly. Families on walks together. Pets seem to be living their best lives with their owners at home all day. Internet yoga. Impromptu cooking lessons online.

This afternoon, after four days of eight-hour-long Zoom meetings, I lay in my bed and watched a silly movie on Netflix and did absolutely nothing. Pure joy!

What does "doing nothing" look like for you?

Joy in Keeping It Together

Social isolation is something I am familiar with as a person who battles depression. Sometimes as a survival mechanism. Sometimes, it is an alert that things are getting really bad. During the pandemic, we were being asked to isolate for our safety. For some, this was a welcomed respite. For others, this was triggering all sorts of anxiety, loneliness, mental instability, and increased depression. Today, we find ourselves faced with some of the same challenges. But now, it is division and difference that seems to separate us. Here are some words of comfort:

> You are not in control of the world around us, but you are in control of YOU.
> Be kind to yourself.
> Take care of yourself.
> Love yourself.
> You are not alone.
> You are loved.
> You are worthy.
> You are more than capable of moving through this.
> Breathe.

How do you keep it all together?

Joy in Quarantine?

"Quarantine": mid-seventeenth century, from the Italian word quarantina ("forty days").

We may not be in quarantine right now, but we have seasons of spiritual quarantines, sometimes self-imposed, other times not. Jesus was tempted in the wilderness for forty days and forty nights. Lent lasts for forty days and forty nights. Those seasons are bearable when we remember that we don't get to Easter morning without the darkness of Good Friday.

"With God's grace, we make a choice to be born anew. It is a choice that changes everything!

We *see* differently.
Our eyes look to the hills from our own life valleys and see that God is the great keeper of our lives! Watching us constantly with us, before us, behind us, beside us. Never slumbering. And we see the divine in everything: in our valleys, in our hilltops, in our enemies, in ourselves.

We *feel* differently.
We feel empowered to completely surrender our lives to God. We exercise a radical obedience, listening for and to God's words, and following them, so ultimately we each may be a blessing to others. We feel free of worry and anxiety because we remember that God already has a dream for our lives, and by righteous faith, we live into that dream, drawing and acting on the divine power and potential that resides deep within us, magnificently woven into our DNA— Emmanuel!

We *act* differently.
We change our ways, our hearts, our minds away from the world and toward God, today. We choose transformation. We choose the story that death is not the end, only a new beginning; that there is always

hope; that wholeness and healing is attainable and that new life and power emerges from the bloodied, beaten, lifeless body of our experiences."

– "Born Anew" in *Becoming Who I Am*

What will you do with your quarantine?

A Winding Road to Joy

"The purpose of a spiritual journey is rarely to find an answer; rather, it is a process of continually asking questions."

– Jessica Elliott, ACC, CEC

When I first wrote these meditations on joy during Lent of 2020, I imagined it would be gaining a deeper sense of what joy means in my life. I was missing it. I yearned for it. But it also seemed the most dissonant and nearly impossible time to learn about joy. The pilgrimage to joy then took on a whole new meaning, with no clear answers.

I was forced to seek out joy at that moment. Or discover the authentic joy inside of me. Joy truly was not easy to find. But I have discovered that I am asking more questions about joy in my life, or rather joy amid life. One thing I have discovered for sure—there is joy in just about anything. We just need the eyes to see it.

As I continue this quest on this spiritual journey of discovery, I am heartened by how God works. The answers are rarely easily seen. Rather, they are revealed in unexpected, unanticipated, and even extraordinary ways. Keep your eyes peeled. Be curious. Ask questions. You never know what you'll discover on this journey called life. And you never know the most unexpected places you can find joy.

> "When going forward in life, it may seem at times overwhelming and unpredictable, resembling more a winding road with many twists and turns. But looking backward, it always seems like a straight line; it makes sense! I was meant to be in those places at those times. Knowing that God has a purpose for my life (Jeremiah 29:11)

keeps me grounded. Knowing that each experience, whether difficult or filled with joy, is an opportunity to learn from and listen to God, gives me confidence, courage, and peace.

Remember forward. Believe backward."

– "Directions" in *Becoming Who I Am*

Where is your road taking you?

What Is Essential for Your Joy?

During the pandemic, we saw this word just about everywhere. Non-essential and essential travel. Non-essential and essential events. Non-essential workers, non-essential workforce, etc. Many of us depended on essential workers.

I constantly asked my children who wanted to leave the house if it was really essential. There was so much fear. So much uncertainty. We realized how much we all took for granted as "essential." We do it now. It makes me think about what is essential for me now. What is truly essential? What is essential for you?

What is essential for your joy? I have discovered that what I know, without a doubt, even when I am most afraid, is that God is faithful and can make wonderful reversals. Especially when we least expect them. With God, death and darkness do not have the last word. Rather, life and light will always make a way. No matter what. That is essential for my joy.

> **"The Lord is my light and my salvation, whom shall I fear? The Lord is the stronghold of my life, of whom shall I be afraid?"**
>
> *– Psalm 27:1 (ESV)*

When I was about thirteen years old and would have bad dreams and couldn't sleep, my father would open the small Bible I had at my bedside to Psalm 27. He would say, "Before you put your head on your pillow, read this psalm and you will not be afraid."

_____

What is essential for your joy?

_____

The Joy of Peace

"It isn't enough to talk about peace. One must be-lieve in it. And it isn't enough to believe in it. One must work at it."

– Eleanor Roosevelt

We are familiar with war zones right now. We know the despair, the lack of hope, and the lack of human dignity. With deep respect for the trauma inflicted on those present in these war zones, I have used war imagery to describe the state of my mind.

I know that I have sought a *peace treaty* in my mind. I yearn for the mental war of words, of self-doubt, of negativity, of equivocation, of not being able to let go, or even self-loathing, to cease … finally. And for a wave of tranquility, self-acceptance, peace, and self-love to flow through.

I expect that there will remain flare-ups in my mental war zone. Sometimes, I cannot even control them. But I am forever surprised and am eternally grateful when new *peace zones* emerge. They seem to be ever-increasing recently. They don't happen on their own. I have to negotiate and navigate these peace treaties consistently.

There is a formula I must follow: part urgent, part courage, part reflection, part diligent work, and a generous dose of forgiveness.

They have yet quite to supplant all the hotspots of conflict-prone areas. But, they are spreading pervasive and contagious elements of peace and tranquility. I feel less afraid, love myself more, and find I'm not that hard on myself. And that, my friend, gives me great hope and joy.

What does your peace feel like?

Joy in Miracles!

Did you know that miracles happen every day? In the most unexpected places, the most unexpected times, even in the simplest actions, even in the moments others take for granted? Miracles are closer to us than we might think. The better we see these miracles, the louder, the brighter, and the more authentic our joy.

The same God who brought sight to the blind
Breathed new life into the dead
Planted babies into barren wombs
Cast demons into pigs
Commended the lame to walk
Fed thousands with little
Halted the flow of disease
Walked on water

Is the same God who
Wake us up each morning
New mercies we see
Breathes new life into the dead marriage
Broken spirit, wounded soul
Plants seeds of opportunities of hope, of help, of grace into
Seemingly infertile situations
Banishes the temptations, the enemies, the bad company
By giving us the will and power to say, "Go!"

Commands us to wake up, get up and choose a new path
Feeds many through willing souls
Unexpected generosity
Kind gestures, acts
Who brings good news in the hospital, new medicines
new cures, new understandings
Miracles surround us every day
Tears that wash away pain

Tears that punctuate joy
A laugh that erupts from our bellies
Touches and hugs that bring comfort and solace
Love that appears in the most unexpected places
Bringing buoyant life, like oxygen to our lungs.

    – "Miracles" in *Becoming Who I Am*

When was your last miracle?

Joy in the Paradox

"This is what God does. God gives his best—the sun to warm and the rain to nourish—to everyone, regardless."

– Matthew 5:45 (MSG)

I am astonished by the great paradoxes in life. That mountaintop and valley experiences coexist, sometimes at the same moment. If we're not careful, we can have spiritual whiplash in witnessing both. How do we hold steady in light of these extremes? Having a deep and abiding joy anchors us. This joy is rooted in God's ever-presence and faithfulness, and it understands that there is meaning and purpose in it all.

From 2020: What happens when you gather a bunch of silly puzzles, boxes of Cracker Jacks, candy, word puzzles, and even some slime—a little "Corona care package" in the middle of isolation? You get two hours of uninterrupted laughter, togetherness, and reconnection even if they are in college and high school (and are more likely to be occupied with proclivities to self-isolate in their headphone musical worlds).

I'm so grateful for a couple hours of togetherness for them and me.

My heart is warmed.

In the not-too-far background, however, I hear the emotional testimony of a nurse who has not hugged her four-year-old daughter for weeks as she fervently protects her family and serves the sick and dying.

My heart is broken.

God is with us all.

What do you do when you see the paradoxes?

Joy in the Seen and Unseen

"We believe in One God ... maker of heaven and earth, of all that is, seen and unseen."
— from the *Nicene Creed*

During the depths of the pandemic, I came to the striking conclusion that,

"It took this unseen contagion for us to see our lives differently."

Pay attention to the seen and unseen. Pay attention to the unseen powerful forces that impact our hearts and minds. Pay attention to the manifestations of those forces that impact how we treat one another. Be open to seeing differently.

Adjust your lens; it is directly connected to your joy.

Sight refocused.

Souls recalibrated.

Interests refreshed.

What we value, reweighed.

Our lives reimagined.

What do you see now?

Joy in Family

> *"How good and pleasant it is when God's people live together in unity!"*
>
> *– Psalm 133:1 (NIV)*

Nothing quite like family. Grateful. Joy-filled. Sweetness.

Our families may look different. They are unique to each of us. Just remember that however your family looks and whomever you choose to be your family, they bring you joy!

_____

Who is your family?

_____

Joy in Power!

That Lent of 2020 was the "Lent-iest" Lent I have ever "Lent-ed"! And I have experienced several "Lent-y" Lents. I've used Lents before as a time to reflect on my story, and in doing so, there are opportunities to turn back some pages, consider new endings, and start new chapters. There is much power and vulnerability in this as I occupy a position of authorship and editor. In it all is a healthy dose of forgiveness, self-love, and courage to see the Good Friday parts of my story with new eyes.

This is what Lent is ... an opportunity for us to keep our eyes on the prize. To rest in the power of the many Lents and Good Fridays we have witnessed and trust that an Easter resurrection awaits us. Now is the time to hold fast, reflect, innovate, shift, forgive, and love harder than we have loved before, knowing that something incredible, unfathomable, and remarkable will occur.

Let's rest in that power! That brings me joy!

What makes you feel powerful?

Joy in Our Good Friday Narratives

We cannot deny the Good Friday narratives of our own lives. What brings me joy is the promise that the death of Jesus is simultaneously the promise of new life and that death does not have the final word! Light and life will make a way.

> *"We are afflicted in every way but not crushed; perplexed but not driven to despair; persecuted but not forsaken; struck down but not destroyed; always carrying in the body the death of Jesus so that the life of Jesus may also be manifested in our bodies."*
> *– 2 Corinthians 4:8–10 (NIV)*

How do you experience joy in your Good Friday moments?

Joy in the In-Between

From time to time, we are all tempted to give up and crumble under the lack of hope. But we are given an awesome gift! The gift of Jesus's resurrection! Knowing that He lives gives us the strength to live through our "Holy Saturday" moments—those moments when our resurrections are uncertain, and our future outcomes remain suspended.

Holy Saturday is that space in between loss and hope, where we don't know if we will ever grasp joy again. In that space, we are called to show up, to stand up, and to look up.

In our soul valley, we are urged to draw close to, desperately hold onto, and embrace God. Now is the time to be courageous, grasp our convictions, and allow the confidence that God will not fail us nor forsake us to fill up our spines and hold us upright as we crawl, walk, and run toward the light of hope!

> *"Trust in the Lord with all your heart and lean not on your own understanding."*
>
> *– Proverbs 3:5 (NIV)*

What do you do in the in-between?

Joy!

Say yes to God's story again today!

Write the healing story into our own life stories and PASS IT ON! Choose to tell the story that laughter will wipe away the tears, light will shatter the darkness, and death is not the end. We are an Easter people! And we cannot be silent. Jesus said that even the stones shall cry out in praise.

So, choose God's story again today! Speak it, sing it, dance it, photograph it, pray it, serve it, write it, work it, heal with it, give it, be it, do it, believe it, tell it.

Say yes to God's story again today and know deep joy!

> *All my life I sing to God*
>
> *Songs of praise*
>
> *Thanksgiving*
>
> *As prayer*
>
> *For God's wonderful reversals!*
>> – "A Spiritual Crescendo" from *Becoming Who I Am*

What parts of God's story do you embrace today?

Bibliography

Engle, Jeremy, *Stress*, Worry and Anxiety Are All Different. How Do You Cope With Each?, *New York Times*, March 11, 2020. (https://www.nytimes.com/2020/03/11/learning/stress-worry-and-anxiety-are-all-different-how-do-you-cope-with-each.html?searchResultPosition=6)

Harvard Business Review, "How to Lead with Purpose", February 11, 2020

Tutu, Desmond and Dalai Lama, *Book of Joy: Lasting Happiness in a Changing World, Random House Publishing, 2016*

Ubuntu, *Internet Encyclopedia of Philosophy: A Peer-reviewed Academic Resource* (https://iep.utm.edu/hunhu-ubuntu-southern-african-thought/)

Wahl, Ellen, *Tai Chi and Qigong, For Centering and Self-Care*, Minneapolis, Minnesota, (https://www.taichiwithellen.com/blog/lotus-love)

Wright, Beth-Sarah, *Becoming Who I Am: Reflections on Wholeness and Embracing Our Divine Stories*, Morehouse Publishing, New York, 2015

Wright, Beth-Sarah, *Ten Things I Wish I Knew About Depression Before it Almost Took My Life*, Lulu Publishing, 2014